CRY BEFORE DAWN

3VSOE000262045

Library of Congress Catalog Card Number 74-15523

ISBN 0-8233-0216-4

75 - 266
1/28/75

Printed in the United States of America

CRY
BEFORE
DAWN

ROBERTA
OLGA
BUTTERFIELD
GOLDSTEIN

THE GOLDEN QUILL PRESS
Publishers

Francestown   New Hampshire

DEDICATED TO FRANK
on our Silver Anniversary
with thanks for 25 glorious years
on our journey to a star, and
a prayer for years to come,
and to our children and grandchildren
with love and hope for those to come!

SHALOM

5735   *1974*

ACKNOWLEDGMENTS

Grateful acknowledgment and thanks are made to the editors of the following magazines and newspapers in which most of these poems first appeared: *The Mountain Troubadour* (Vermont), *The Guild* and the *Poets' Guild* (Idaho), *Poet* (India), *Cyclo-Flame* (Texas), *Imprints Quarterly* (New York), *The Jewish Spectator* (New York), *Jewish Information* (Chicago, Ill.), *Ocarina* (India), *Cahier de Poésie* (C.S.S.I., Rome, Italy), *Encore* (New Mexico), *Poetry Prevue* (New York), *Driftwood* (Rhode Island), *Memorabilia Anthology* (Arkansas), *Poets' Guild Anthology* (Idaho), *Mitre Press Spring Anthology* (London, England), *The Rutland Herald* (Vermont), *South West Times Record* (Arkansas), *The Cahokia Herald, Dupo Herald Tribune* and *New Athens Journal Press* (Illinois), *The Hartford Courant* (Connecticut).

Special permission received from Asch Recordings to reprint "Wall of Destiny," copyright Asch Recordings, 1970.

Grateful thanks to Rocco Ruggiero (Rock Rogers) for reading many of these poems on his program "A Tribute to Poets" WBTN (Bennington, Vt.).

To our daughter, Ethel-Faith, a million thanks for secretarial assistance beyond the call of filial duty.

CONTENTS

CRY BEFORE DAWN

WAITING FOR A CRY

Before the word
there was the cry!
The inarticulate,
struggling to stand erect,
rent the seams of heaven
with his cry.
Before the song
there was the cry
of angels
too awestruck
to murmur words.

Before his Creator
man knelt dumb,
yet from the depths
of his humility
uttered the first
fluted vowel.

Now after billions
and billions of lavish,
rhetorical words
   and meaningless slogans,
   the Great Producer
   waits in the wings
   of the Theater
   of the Absurd
   and listens for
   one human cry
   telling him that man
   still remembers why. . .

BENEATH THE GLASS

Here in my plush, plump tangerine chair,
I watch the raindrops slithering by
My eyeglass world of angles and squares,
While the heavens cry, I sit dry eyed.
Yet somewhere the skies are raining flame,
Rockets and eggs of lethal lead, —
It doesn't matter to them in Whose Name
The silver taloned eagles fly,
Their sky has fallen, their earth is red.

No insulation can surround the soul,
It burns and bleeds from a brother's pain,
An eyeglass world lies sane and cold,
While the inner eye sees worlds insane.

CRY BEFORE DAWN

Man! Woman! Lovingly sculptured
in MY Image
amid the wealth
of forests, streams and seas,
My patience withers.
The creatures of the Ark
dwindle down too fast
the song of the lark
no longer lifts
in exultation;
the Rainbow —
seal of our Covenant —
rises invisible
to smoke drugged eyes.
The robots stalk
through cities clogged
with living death
and an affluence of pain.

What fruit can they pluck —
My Innocents
whose birthright
has been exchanged
for nuclear pottage?
Through the darkness
of the tunnel
where you now slouch
in fitful slumber,
crawl toward the light!
Cry, cry before dawn breaks

in fiery splendor
on some infant planet
where you are *not*!

NOT EVEN SEVEN VEILS

Once more my eyes behold
the olive limbs of April
undulating
beneath her seven veils.
Her breath warm as the womb
scents the air I breathe —
I smell crushed violets.
My senses cannot resist
the unwavering gaze
of green eyes that offer
the gift of rebirth.
Yet suddenly I hear
The slow roll of drums, —
the vision of April fades.
Even her seven veils
cannot hide the red blood
inundating
the rivers of the world.

RING OUT THE GLORY

And all the bells ring out my love,
and all the bells ring out
as the curtain falls
on the denouement of the drama,
that a penniless poet,
scribbling in blood,
entitled "Insanity."
In vain I look into the eyes
of listless soldiers
returning from the mud.
No mellow tones enthrall my ears,
only the immensity
of hollow silence.
I move, encased in ice,
to embrace a phantom
whose shattered skull
lies within a tomb
alien to my limbs.
Crumbling bones can never bear
my gift of flesh.
Your bones bleach white, my love,
in lime kiln glory
to the pealing of the bells,
And I walk forward blindly —
alone in my frozen caul —
to live forever
in the halls of hell.

A TEEN-AGER ASKS WHY

"Man lives by faith and not by bread alone."
The steel grey eyes of the preacher smiled
as he closed the Holy Book. "Remember this,
Isaac did not flinch or moan when Abraham
once bound him fast upon the altar stone."

In the rear pew a teen-age boy pondered
the meaning within the story.
His brow furrowed in quizzical thought
as he sought to recapture history
with the camera of his inner eye, —
a kaleidoscopic wheel turned in the limbo
between heaven and hell.

There stood Abraham, knife in hand,
suspended for one soundless moment!
The sun paused in its orbit
as from the thicket a white ram ran, —
a living miracle to receive the blade!
Abraham loosened the bonds of his son
and tears mingled with rivulets
of blood from the ram of redemption.

The teen-age boy asked himself this question:
"Is this fantasy or faith?
Somewhere does a God exist without hunger
for the taste of human flesh?"
The boy trembled as he beheld the drama
of men moving through moon-mad centuries
to the limits of outer space.

Time churned in the lens of the camera
and dirt whirled to the rhythm
of tramping feet. The blood of human sacrifice
drenched the breast of earth.

Mothers and Fathers kissed their sons
and praised their names as they went forth
to bind their bodies upon the altars
where fires once burned
to Astarte, Moloch, and Baal.

The boy ran from his pew and leaped to the pulpit.
The lightning of his breath
shattered the windows of stained glass;
the cathedral choir hushed the Gloria
and the congregation smothered its "Amen."
"Why?" he demanded, "Why do my brothers die?
Has Satan slaughtered all the rams of heaven?
Or has man at last moulded his God
in the image of human clay?"

VIVE LA FRANCE

Au revoir, Charles, mon Général,
adieu to a fallen god.
I remember the golden nimbus
encircling your head
when you, erect and tall,
strode into the cracked shell
of *ma belle France*.
"Vive Charles, vive DeGaulle,
Vive, Vive la France."
You stepped like a giant, —
we knelt to kiss the flaming sod
where your ten league boots
struck tinder in Parisian mud.
The decades pass; icons slip.
Your vision was too infinite
for mortal man to grasp.
A thunderbolt!
For you, Olympian oblivion.
Alone in the country you still stabbed
the heart of history with your pen.
Would that men had been less fickle,
but we are born to topple the very gods
that we once mounted on the pedestal.
"A hero never feels the kiss of death
but once. *Vive, vive la France."*

"WE DEEPLY REGRET TO INFORM YOU"

Dearest Kenneth,
I received the telegram today
at the precise moment when April
kissed the earth with her violet mouth,
here on your own New England hills.
I came here to gather trillium and anemones,
Jack-in-the-pulpit and adder tongues,
as we always did when the sun grew ripe.
Now, strangely lost, I wander
in grottos of silence
unbroken by the echo of your laughter.
Beyond the woods, our grassy knoll
feels alien to my touch.
The phantom who walks with me
exudes a frigid breath,
unlike the warmth of you who gave me life.

A keening cry knifes the crust
of my loneliness. I leap
through the hoop of the vernal equinox —
as sun turns the newborn buds
of oak and ash to lemon lime.
Somewhere the church bells peal
a bridal-funeral chime.
Suddenly the flood gates open!
The rain drenches me,
and through the rain I see
a million hollow eyes, dull as burnt out coal.
They stare at me from every branch
of every mourning tree.

The white anemones turn crimson
at my leaden feet.
I hear the slow roll of drums,
the endless bark of guns,
and the beat of soldiers' hearts.
I see a rain of blood — a rain of death.
Now comes the rain of bleeding leaves,
and the rain of fire!
I walk in rain that sears my soul.

And if a miracle should appear
as did the dove to Noah,
how can I bring forth my greening shoot
without the sower of the seed?
                    Your loving wife,
                         Lenore

CHRISTMAS CANDLE BIRTHDAY

It was my sixteenth year of seasoning,
and the skies were frosted with sugar stars;
the wind blew glitter on my birthday cake,
and I thought my Christmas candle birthday
might last through the fourth of July.
Father covered me with his buffalo robe,
and we rode in the sleigh in the spangled snow.
The harness bells jingled my birthday song, —
they sang of the day when flowered and veiled,
I would marry the gentle prince, riding
on the far side of the crystal mountain
on his moonstone unicorn.
The prince wore the same face that was reflected
by the morning mirror when my father shaved.
The eyes of the prince smiled like my father's
when he looked at his only daughter.
The horses tossed their manes in the icy air,
and the bells shook their silver hallelujahs.
Our breath curled in blue-white smoke,
yet, I felt as warm as if I were kneeling
beside the tree, and eagerly waiting
to open the gifts, tied with love knots,
from a Kris-Kringle-Father-Prince.

FROM THE HEART OF THE ROCKET

The intrepid three swung in orbit,
Cycling around and around,
Glimpsing what man had never seen
The secret, dark side of the moon.
No welcome issued from the silent orb
Immersed in the hush of solitude.
The pioneers looked out with pride
At the blue ball, their faithful planet,
And from the rim of the unknown,
They chose to send this Christmas message:

> "In the beginning God created
> The Heaven and Earth. . .
> And God said: 'Let there be light'
> And there was light."

Somewhere on the blue ball, a guest
Arose from the holiday table,
And toasted that awestruck moment
When Adam and Eve, knowing good and evil,
Began man's long pilgrimage
From the Garden of Eden
To the dark of the moon,
And many stars beyond.

SERMONS IN STONE

The old order falters —
prayers and marches
replaced by
gunfire and hostages.
The frenzied drummer
sets a fast tempo
a machine gun answers
with staccato spray.
Passion juices once
bottled and corked
erupt and spew
purple acid.
Mint julep Senators
thunder on
while blood turns wine
in the waiting.
The battle lines
form in the cities.
The unconcerned
sit on plush cushions
hypnotized
by the idiot box
whose voice muffles
the crescendo of thousands,
once unpitchforked,
now pulling down
stone by stone
the white Bastille!

CANDLE THE DARK

Blow winds, blow the cobwebs
from my mind,
tear into shreds
the dusty, shuttered blinds
that keep my eyes
from seeing
my brothers
in iron chains.
Let my ears receive the cries
of the mothers
who find no grain
to glean from fields
once swollen with wheat;
their golden yield
now sickled
and ground
as the hammers beat.
Here lies the land
of their nativity,
a banquet
for the corpulent body
of the State.
Let me ignite a spark,
one candle that breaks
the friendless dark!

JAN MASARYK SPEAKS
(March 10, 1968)

The raven decades have flown over my grave,
and always I have waited impatiently, yet
faithfully, for the mountain Říp to open,
and the plumed knights with lancers poised,
to gallop forth on chargers and chase
the invader from our beloved soil.
I shall not rest in peace while hammers
beat against the hearthstone of my country;
too long have sickles flailed the sinews
and stripped the marrow of our spirit.
With crumbling bones I have nourished
the last feeble flame of liberty that sprang
from my father's loins into the womb
of our mother Czechoslovakia.
I did not choose to leap from life to death
and abandon you, my people, in your agony,
but the Deceiver plunged me into the abyss
of anonymity, and erased the name of Masaryk
from the hallowed history of our Republic.
For twenty lonely years only the rain and snow
remembered me. Living men who sleep without
a dream must endure the nightmare, but in death,
my candle flares against the dark.

II
Now on the twentieth anniversary of my death,
you have come, my people, you have come
to comfort me with the salt of your sorrow.
You have opened the ancient stronghold Říp,

and have marched to my forbidden grave
with the white plumes of your courage, the iron
of your unconquerable will, and your gift of love.
In your blue jeans and turtlenecks, and your
Sunday suits, you look more radiant
than warriors in glittering armor.
My dream rises through flagstone to your throats.
You shout our National Anthem! In your hands
you hold the "Lightning Above The Mountain."
Above your chant of liberation, I hear again
the rumble of enemy tanks,
and the noise of alien commands.
Lift up your hearts, my people, I pledge
that I will wait until the redemption
when the bones of the family Masaryk
shall rest in the soil of a free Republic!

FLIGHT TO SANITY

She knew they whispered behind her back,
that she was mad
as a March hatter,
but it didn't matter to her
that these matronly marionettes
of Suburban Siberia
would never perceive
that she was not a candidate
for the analyst's couch.
A casualty of hate and ennui,
she simply walked away
one Friday afternoon
from the chatter of mudpie parties,
and the smoke of weekend barbecues.
When her handsome, pole-climbing husband
discovered one cocktail hour
that his showpiece was missing,
the wooden jaws made quite a clatter.
No one would ever have concluded
that she left to seek her lost soul,
and found it one day in the hot,
antiseptic interior
of a hospital ward
as she tightly held
a soldier's hand.

WHAT DOES SEPTEMBER?

September burns like a bonfire
melting the frost
with tangerine flames.
September spins a carousel
of pinto ponies
with tawny manes;
it's a carnival of thieves,
of hucksters and knaves;
it's a festive fair
where Indian maidens
with supple arms
and dusky hair,
barter their yield
of saffron kisses.
September sways like a gypsy
to the rhythm
of tambourines,
as a pumpkin lantern
gleams through the haze.
The school bell peals a summons
to the laggards
still at play,
while wild ducks fly
across the canvas
of a burnt orange sky.
September spills doubloons
of pirate gold,
and those who share it
never grow old!

WIN OR LOSE

Not with calculated hatred
or careful premeditation
did she cuckold her husband,
she was only playing the game.
Her paramour played for high stakes,
and he always played to win.
Win or lose, all she could feel
was the high voltage thrill
of a gambler's risk.
One night he neatly piled his chips
into one towering stack,
then with a puckish grin
gave her the honor.
Her choice was black!
The Wheel spun and stopped,
the House had lost;
they drank to Lady Luck.
Later, gleaming with fire-struck
diamonds, and swinging her sable,
she pranced into his plush stable.
Two floors below, her husband,
weary of betting on the wrong horse,
finally blew his horns off, —
along with his brains, of course.

ONCE IN SPLINTERED SUNLIGHT

The thunder of the pipe organ
swelled to a stop —
down stone steps in silence
fluttered the mourning doves
into glass sunlight,
then, chatter churned the air
as doves turned magpies,
forgetful of the gadfly's sting.
As they flew into nests
of woven steel
the deserted street
lay mourning
while the oaken box,
arrayed with lilies,
was borne by sturdy penguins
to the entrails of the raven;
jet wings dipped farewell
in the splintered sunlight, —
one swift ascent
before the last descent
into the hungry mouth
of April earth.

THE PRINCESS OF MAKE-BELIEVE

When I was young and the world was tall,
There were lovely lollypop trees;
A yellow balloon sailed around the skies,
And pirates combed over the silky seas.

My palace of glass had a fifty foot hall
Where I danced with my white-plumed prince;
We waltzed all night over mirror bright floors
Then dined on a thimble of quince.

When I was young and troubles were small,
There were orchards of sugar plums;
A noisy blue jay screamed thief-thief,
And a woodpecker played the drums.

When I was young the world was a ball,
A Crystal Ball that reflected *me* —
The prince always moved at my command,
No one dared spurn my royal decree.

Then the Crystal Ball cracked and fell,
My prince rode off to the wicked town,
My hands kept bleeding from bits of glass
As the palace walls came tumbling down.

ONCE THERE WAS FIRE

I feel the first blood-red leaf
of September
fall on my hungry hand,
and I remember
the shimmering sheaf
of ripened wheat
that we shared in brief,
incandescent moments,
when the drums of morning
with pattering beat
made us dance —
until the earth began
to burn beneath our feet.
The bonfires of autumn
flared with an August heat!
Now the drums are hushed,
and unseen bagpipes
skirl your elegy.
No fire lightens my grief,
no harvest grain
fills my granary.
All I hold
is this fallen leaf
with its bleeding vein
of memory.

TONGUE IN CHEEK DELIVERY
TO THOSE WHO CAN'T STOP

Up, up the spiral staircase
of the driven day,
do not hang forever
on the ladder
of the night.
Climb, climb
toward galaxies of light.
Never stop to swing
on the trapeze
at the fair.
Run, run up the curves,
gasping, gasping
for each breath.
Strain, strain
toward the purest air!

Let no man bind you
to a rock,
nor woman chain you
to a clock.
You were not born
to grovel on the ground,
soar, soar beyond
supersonic sound,
Up, up the spiral staircase
of the shriven day.

WHAT DOES OCTOBER?

October is a jack o'lantern
lighting the dusk
with a rakish grin.
October plays a carillon
ringing in rhythm.
It's a silken husk
of crimson and gold
covering the hilt
of a flashing sword.
October is a broken V
of wild geese that scream
as they plummet to earth,
while hunters beam
in their snug blinds
beneath a sky
of falling down.
October wears the mask
of a tear-stained clown
who shivers to feel
his frozen frown.
It's a faded love song,
an autumnal dirge,
yet can speak with the tongues
of ten brass gongs
to the resilient ears
of the young!

THE GIFT OF FIRE

You warmed me with Promethean fire
When all my limbs were fettered
In the cavern of the night.
You scaled the palace of desire
When tall frozen tapers
Mocked the inner sight.
Encircled by an ice capped moat
I lay, dreamless in a dungeon,
With chains for prayer beads.
You leaped across the icy flood
To burn the glacier in my throat,
I felt the surge of warming blood
As you gave my body liberty
And poured your fire over me.

The gift of fire, once purloined
From the niche where false gods dwell,
Bestows upon mortal man
A legacy of death;
And thus it was with you, Prometheus,
Your tryst with fire kindled
Freedom torches throughout the land.
Then the twisted Furies
With poisonous fangs
Extinguished your breath.
Your body lies on a barren cliff
Where vultures peck your ember eyes,
Your hand
   that cupped the light will never
Lift my most un-nuptial veil.

My flesh curls in ashes of desire,
Yet my spirit rises purified,
A disembodied bride,
Whose shadow moves within your fire.

DEDICATED TO THE PRESERVATION
OF WONDER

When my daughter was a little girl,
she tossed aside her dolls,
football and kickball
were more her style.
Boys were alive
and much more fun
than playing house
without them.
Fifteen years have fled,
now she is twenty
and recipient of
two Raggedy Annes on the bed
staring open-eyed
at a velvet puppet,
and a calico frog
(not yet turned prince)
great glass eyes blinking
while a merry-go-round
plays tinkling tunes.
Spilling over the shelves
in every nook
are the children's classics
and well handled books
of long gone generations.
These are the gifts
selected with careful dedication
by young men who feel
the wonder of childhood
must be preserved
if man's survival
is worth the struggle.

THE PILGRIMAGE

I went back home today
where mountains stretch
their brawny arms
to capture sun.
I walked along the path
where phantoms glow
with the Promethean fire
that burned me whole.
I found the hidden spring
that filled our cup
with crystal mead,
when we ruled side by side
upon the emerald throne
of Avalon.
Now misty kingdoms float
within the eye
of scarlet tanagers
who shared our summer
paradise. The mountains lift
their sunlit torch
above your bed of dust
while echoes mock
my pilgrimage.
I drain my cup
and taste the liquid salt.

OF POODLES AND PUDDLES

I looked at a Chicken Little scene
The sky was falling in!
I spied Henney Penney
Hopping through the splashing raindrops,
her feet snug in yellow plastics
and her bare head bobbling around
above a Kelley green raincoat.
The black poodle with floppy ears
showed no alarm about the falling sky,
there he was dragging Henney Penney
slipping and skidding over the slick grass
(holding on to his leash for dear life)
(holding on to his leash for her very life)
straight to his private puddling place
under a stately umbrella of elms.

THE PROMISE

There is somewhere deep inside
where I can not intrude,
I sense your innate need
for a core of solitude,
and promise never to invade
or touch one single seed.

First let me taste the fruited tang
of the crisp outer skin,
and I'll respect your yin and yang
and will not enter in.

SCULPTURED LOVE

You brushed my cheek
with falcon wings,
and gave my fingers
emerald rings.
You stroked my lips
with a mailed glove
and cleft my chin
with chiseled love.

You moulded me
like sculptor's clay
and shaped me in your
flawless way,
but my soul defies
your magic art
and love lies locked
within my heart.

NOVEMBER CELLOS

November cellos moaned their hollow elegies,
The wind lamented like a keening crone;
Stacatto rain tatooed the naked trees, —
Bereft of human touch, I mourned alone.
As dry dead leaves clung feebly to the oak,
And autumn mists obscured the telltale spark
Of bonfires, spicing night with pungent smoke,
You came to find me in the coffin-dark.
You wore no shining armor or white plume,
Nor were you riding on a milk white mare;
No flower of knighthood in full bloom
Ever could have offered such sterling ware.

Tonight I hear November cellos singing, —
Like them I move from grieving to Thanksgiving!

CINNAMON AND CLOVE

You in the kitchen
creating fresh pumpkin pies
cinnamon and clove
bubbling mincemeat
simmering applesauce
amber autumn days
pungent
enticing
perfumed
rolling into nights
of spicy sheets
cinnamon and clove
the scent of love
and you.

WITHIN HIS SECRET HEART

Those tasteless, tactless grown-ups once remarked:
"How very handsome you would look, young man,
if only your unruly locks were shorn."
Not choosing to offend his elders,
he slew them with his Huck Finn grin.

What might they see if they could peer
within the sanctum of his room?
This teen-ager of rock and roll —
who wears worn corduroy pants
with modish velvet jackets —
now satisfies his hungry soul.
Through the magnetic power of thought,
an old oil painting transports him
to the towering spires of Camelot.
Enraptured by the magic of Merlin,
and dubbing no knight as brave as Lancelot,
he vows to play the more tragic role
of Arthur, most chivalrous of fabled heroes.

Although the electronic tune of the steel guitar
has usurped the minstrel lute, still deep
within his secret heart there flows
the runic rhythm that the poets taught
in the shining palace of Camelot.

CAN YOU ENTER?

What do you know of children?
What do you know of hope?
Do you know how to blend
starlight stories
with the blue trumpets
of morning glories,
or do you only linger
in the garden of darkness
where purple foxgloves dwell?
Do you shiver in silence
and fear you cannot cope
with the twisted roots
of "the not quite whole"
who grow beyond your scope?
Can you love the "slow bloomers,"
and your heart understand
the world of young dreamers,
whose fate you now hold
like a rose in your hand?
Are you only a miser
existing for gold,
or can you enter
the kingdom of children
on sandals of silver?
There your eyes will behold
the souls of the flawed
kindled and glowing
like the candles of God!

ONCE IN A VELVET DREAM

Nut brown hair piled high
like a royal crown
upon a princess' head,
she sits
cross-legged
like a little girl
upon her bed
in a long purple gown
and twists a curl.
A clock purls the hour —
hoofbeats echo!
She runs to the window
and sees only
bare branches
scraping the crusty snow.
Surprise arches
dusky eyebrows,
she sighs impatiently
and returns
to her velvet dream.
Eyes close, head nods
as if to affirm
the certain coming
of Lancelot.

DREAM BEFORE THE DAWN

Thirty-three summers have plummeted down,
thirty-three green apple springs have dried,
thirty-three winters have scattered their snow
as thirty-three autumns spiralled in smoke.
Yet in the hushed hour before the dawn
I dreamed of you, my father,
in all your brawny prime.
I saw your eyes smokey blue
like a hazy autumn sky,
and heard your lips speak the words
for which my heart hungered.
Then you held out your strong, firm hands
that once held a surgeon's scalpel.
When I awoke to the morning clock
and the whirr of the working world,
my dream had vanished with the sun,
but your healing hands have made me whole
once again; I will not be a coward.

Still one question like a broken record
repeats and repeats in my brain:
"When my bones have been seasoned like timber
by thirty-three winters, springs, summers,
and fire-laden autumns, what dreams
will my dear children choose to dream
in their own hushed hour before the dawn?"

TO MY DAUGHTER

Child of yesterday, woman of tomorrow,
you will linger but a moment on the rim
of maidenhood. Then you will cross over —
beyond my hungry reach.
My anxiety for your future spirals,
since we live in a time-space where
footprints of crisis loom larger
than those of the Abominable Snowman.
I would give you an amulet to guard you
against the witches of darkness,
but must not look back, or like the faithless
spouse of Lot, I, too, may turn to salt.
You must forge the links for your own armor
with the malleable metal of love. Your lance
may be a laser beam that penetrates
the stockpile of hate.

II

What crumbs of wisdom can I throw in your path?
You are not a sparrow depending on the compassion
of a human heart for your survival.
You and your peers may counsel the parliament
of nations as we begin the long night's journey
into the eldorado of peace.
I put on sackcloth and ashes for we, your elders,
have given you a world, wrapped in tinfoil, that
    clicks
like a time bomb. I pray to the One Force,
be he called Jehovah, Allah, Buddha, Krishna,
Christ, or the Nameless Light, that you,

51

the galactic generation, may defuse
the sadistic mechanism before the birthday
cake of earth crumples into cinder crumbs.
My child, I can give you nothing, but
the smouldering core of my faith!

AND RUSTIC EDENS

The odor of shaving soap and the masculine
fragrance of you still lingered
in the red barn. Even the smell of freshly
mown hay did not cancel your scent.
A covey of thrush skimmed in and out
of the pitching hole, and sang with hearts
that would not be denied the full
expression of melodic joy.
How could I ask them to convert
luminous alleleuias into a widow's elegy?

Thrusting back cries of self-pity caught
in my throat, I sought to savor once more
the purple clover moments shared
in the red barn, our sanctum
from the carnival beyond the hill.
Craving more than the loaf I gave,
more than peace garnered too seldom,
you left. I wonder if you sought
to gain a portion of that Greater Love
Who carved mountains, restless men,
and rustic Edens?

AND THEN THERE'S FEBRUARY

February shakes a quiver
of zinging arrows
from Cupid's bow
trailing scarlet ribbons
scattering sunset glow.
February blossoms daily
with intimate nosegays
of purple blue violets
in a lace paper doily.

February embroiders
soft silken twilights
with mauve mist floss
rolling off lakes and rivers.
February spins a legend
of log cabin
and cherry tree —
tall amethyst shadows
the turning of a key
the slow opening
of long locked doors.

February ends with a song
floating from violins
for lovers who lie
heart pressed to heart
under the orchid sheet
of lavender scented sleep —
never more than a breath apart.

WHISPERING LEAVES

Upon the silent furnaces
and slumbering chambers,
where six million martyred Jews
chanted their prayer of faith,
the silver leaves still fall.
Their words, *ani ma 'amin*, uttered
before the forest was stripped
of trees with burgeoning buds,
still echo from silver leaves.
The shadow of "mashiah"
lengthens upon the western wall.
He may yet come to shake
the citadels of Pharaohs,
who once again devise plans
to deprive the surviving forest
of sun and chlorophyll.
When will our brother's keeper
heed the whispering
of silver leaves,
once green with April hope?

AND SO IT SHALL BE DONE

Each man in his generation
must encounter new Pharaohs
who seek to build still loftier
pyramids with blood and bones
for brick and mortar.
Lean Pharaohs hunger
to mount upon the altar
their stone-hewn images,
and etch in hieroglyphics
their fameless names.

Each man in his generation
must surrender to the lash
of sickled whips and bow low
before the icons, or cast
the images asunder, —
destroy the sceptered hammer,
and unlock the chain
of every slave!

As he walks erect from bondage
like a prince to freedom born,
his restless feet must wander
over the shifting sand,
onward and ever upward,
until he scales the rocks
of Sinai and communes
with the Holy One.

THE WALL OF DESTINY

The copper gong of the mid-east sun
and the brass tongues of
sputtering guns splinter
the air of Jerusalem. A soldier,
oblivious of the dissonance,
rejoices like a lost son
restored to the sanctity of home.
Tears mingle with sweat on his
grimy, unshaven face as he leans
against the remnant of the temple
and chants his love song:
"Wall of memories, stained with
the tears of pilgrims and the blood
of my people; fortress of the human
heart that has prevailed through two
thousand years as a changeless
symbol of hope on the ever
changing map of a shrinking world,
I have kept my rendez-vous."

Bullets quiver like poison arrows
in the blue-black smoke as he gently
caresses the blazing stones like a
bridegroom on the first night
with his beloved.
Time freezes like an alabaster
statue, and death poises
on the precipice of history!
He prays and hears six million times
six million voices echo

57

from the valley of dry bones
and the ashes of fiery furnaces.
The twisted cross and the scimitar —
crescent dissolve like figments
of an alien nightmare.

The soldier sees with a poet's eyes
the fruit of reality
born from the wombs
of the daughters of Zion.
The exile has returned from the hot sands
of the desert where the bush burned
but refused to be consumed.
He pours cool water from Jacob's well
over the arid breast of stone,
and with the lips of a poet
he seals his love for the Holy One.

A stray bullet strikes his heart!
His blood flows freely
as he scrawls upon the wailing wall —
his final declaration
of immortality!

WHAT IS JUNE?

June is a melody
floating from organs
and calliopes,
from cellos and oboes.
June is a medley, —
a swish of white dresses
down flowered aisles,
buttercup kisses
and garlands of daisies;
the quicksilver smiles
of half adolescents,
quite sure that the nation
shall prevail
when their generation
swings the tiger
by its tail.
June is a tear in the eye,
and a lump in the throat;
a time of good-byes,
the beginning of hope!
June sounds a tympany
with cymbal and drum;
June is a lover's
rhapsody.

TOO LONG REMEMBERING

Tonight in your anger, my daughter,
you chanced to move the slivers
of my glass blown illusions. Again,
I heard the clash of crystal chimes,
and saw lightning flashing
in the sky of my high noon.
Now you vow to carve your design
from the phantom ivory of dreams.
When he comes, the one with whom
you will reign in your forever
kingdom, can you cut him
in the pattern of your Prince?
Living, loving, apart from
the madding mob and mock ritual,
(you assume) will fill your cup
with nectar. You swear no sinister
knave of fate will trip you up.

I could tell you how dreams wear thin,
even snap from the weight of time,
but I sit mute as a cloistered nun —
eyelids swollen from too long remembering
the knife-bright pain
of slivering illusion.

BEHIND THE BATTLE LINES

Once I knew not any war
nor destruction;
I held no fear
only your child
within the warmth
of my body,
and the rain of leaves
sang us lullabies.
But, oh, today
when my time has come,
the rain of the leaves
is mid-wife and husband.
I bear my lonely labor
and listen as the rain
of leaves mingles
with the crackling thunder
of alien guns.
My blood congeals
as rain drips red
against my eyelids.

A comrade comes with love
from my dying soldier.
"Sleep gently, my husband,
your son with lusty cry
is born upon our bed; —
the reign of death
suspended."

"ALL LIFE IS A PARTING. . ."

We talked ourselves out that gusty night
stuck in a snowbank
in full view of the cemetery.
Looking at snow mantled stones, you said:
"Our mates lie dead. . . but I know
I still have a body. . . how about you?"
(Purely a rhetorical question, you knew
the voracious appetite of the widowed;
I was not less hungry or less cold
than you, my black Irishman).
Like mendicants sharing a loaf of bread,
and a bottle of strong red wine,
we shared the warmth of each other.

Afterwards, we kept in touch, but never again
such blessed communion.
I married. You left abruptly.
Long years, lean with scribbled cards —
and on your rare visits to town —
dark smiles and half-stilted conversation.
Then, the breaking headline of your death!
I cried, remembering how tightly,
you and I once held to a lifeline
that storm tossed night
outside the cemetery.

SONG AND LIGHT

Today the dawn broke
like a soft boiled egg
spilling its yolk
in the China blue
of my empty bowl.
The coffee bubbled
without spilling over
and the canary
untroubled
by his bars
swang and sang
a high keyed
love song.

Assaulted by song
and light, could I
do less than end
my long night's weeping?
I felt and heard
my hard shell
crisply breaking
and *joie de vivre*
awakening!

FIRST SPRING

This is the first spring for Juliana,
who is flowering
like the pink and white petals
on the apple trees
in her grandfather's orchard.
The silk crowning her head
blows yellow gold
like the budding forsythia.
Juliana moves with fingers curved
to catch the flecks of sun,
her bare feet dance
through the open morning
of her first birthday,
and the plum and pear trees
shower her with white fragrance.
Looking out from eyes
blue as a clean swept sky,
Juliana sings
her song of jubilation,
and the greening earth
spins in celebration!

BLACK IS BEAUTIFUL

Black is the cradle of the stars,
rocked by the breath of night.
Black is the undying rose
that your fingers etched
on pale parchment.
Black as a rare orchid is love,
and deep as a mountain pool
in the hour before dawn.
Black is your supple flesh
like polished ebony,
and black is your glossy hair
like the wings of a mynah bird.
Black is my carved teakwood chest,
where swathed in thin black tissue,
lies my velvet bridal dress.
You are mine, belovéd, —
black and beautiful and pure!

A MINOR MIRACLE

Like delicate white violets
the snowflakes swirl
outside our castle wall.
We lie quietly inside
sharing a minor miracle
on the white fur rug
beside a strawberry fire.
Insulated for tonight
by banks of white flowers,
we can ignore
the tug of war.
It's not hard to evade
the savage hate outside
when we hold each other close
in a universe of light —
pulsing with wonder!

GOLDEN LOOPS

After the desert of the day
comes an oasis of love and light
     the chatter of ice
     in moving
          liquid
     the twilight hour
     dealing
          conversation
     just we four
     a decade apart
     yet suiting
          each other
     matching
          kings and queens —
I and you, younger brother,
bound by our blood line,
and to chosen partners
by sons and daughters
glowing
          golden and precious
as this fire leaping
               in the room
linking
     the four of us
          in loops
of laughter!

LOVE LADEN HANDS

I shall not wait until your eyelids close
To spill my tears upon your inert breast,
Or place within your hand one crimson rose.
Before the sun surrenders to the west,
I shall arrive with laurel laden hands
And set upon your brow a victor's crown.
You do not fear the glass of running sands,
Nor do you moan when golden leaves fall down.
Your feet have often sped through storm and fire
To share the loaf of wisdom with a friend.
You play such melodies upon the lyre,
I can not bear to know the songs will end.

Yes, I will give you all my love this day,
And not remember that "all must pass away."

UNAFRAID

Perhaps our love was never young
like the first tender bloom
upon the flowering plum.
It tasted more like fruit ripened
under a truant August sun —
semi-sweet yet tingling tart.
Now twenty-two years have aged our tree,
the plums are falling fast;
we gather the late autumn harvest
unafraid of the final decree.
We know our love is fit
for any eternity.

WITH PERFECT TRUST

I am the soil that holds
the seed and shell of life;
In the violet twilight
I sense the April thrust
and know His Hand has blessed
my common dust.

I am the meadow lark
whose song electrifies
the sky with liquid light;
I soar to golden peaks
then wheel and glide to earth
with perfect trust.

I am the man who died
to give his sons their chance
to grow, to learn to love;
My bones have turned to chalk
although my soul has cleft
tinsel wrapped clod.

I am my mother's child,
my father killed in war,
flesh lost in battle smoke;
yet I know that somewhere
in space beyond the dark
he lives with God.

KINDLING LIGHT

I travel backwards in the time tunnel
to seek again that looking glass
where our faces still smile
with the joy of rain-soaked children
coming suddenly upon a dry cabin.
In a world where part of our people
had spiralled into grey smoke
that hardened into cold stars,
we found each other. Together
we were no longer refugees —
no longer flotsam that survived
the eye of the hurricane.
In each other's eyes we glimpsed
a blue-green flame like the light,
kindling a wooded mountain,
when the sun has ridden out
Above the storm.

MY YAFFAH, MY SHAINE

Come Avramle, my only brother,
Come out of the sky
Where you play your bass viol
Upside down on the purple roofs
Of our vanished village.
I, alone, crept out alive
From Aunt Frieda's cellar
Where you hid me weeping
Among the turnip and cabbage.
Come, Avramle, see with my eyes,
See the daughter of Mordecai ben Ephraim
Dancing and leaping!
Like a grasshopper she jumps
To the beat of our pulse,
Her hair shaking like rippling wheat!
She is my Shaine, my Yaffah, my Pretty One.

She dances like all the Pretty Ones
We loved in our childhood --
All lost to the sky like our village.
But Yaffah lives!
Yaffah, blonde as wild honey,
Eyes blue as our mother's best china,
Her pounding feet trample the Aryan myth.
Like our nightingale in the ghetto,
My three year old grandchild sings:
"Dovid melek Yisrael — chai, chai!"
She claps her hands,
Stomps her bare feet,

Her white teeth shining
In the light of the candles.

Avramle, do you hear them?
All the others — singing,
Their voices blending
With the sweet voice of my Shaine?
They sing with her as we sang
Together, when children
On the Sabbath of our village.

My Yaffah, my Shaine, my Pretty One dances!
She leaps like a gazelle,
She skips like a spring lamb,
Her upturned face cups the Sabbath Delight!
Her song, her laughter heal the old wounds,
Her "ruach" melts the stones of the ovens.

Come, Avramle, hold my hand,
And the hand of the others,
All the Pretty Ones dance and sing
With my Yaffah, my Shaine,
And even the Baal Shem Tov laughs again!

THE TAPESTRY OF GOLD
(In Memoriam: Sister Mary Ambrose)

With a touch of Midas the October sun
sifted through glass and gilded
your hospital room
until even the mirror reflected
a sparkle of Spanish doubloons;
and the vase that held the season's
first bouquet of bittersweet
glittered with luminescence.
Skeins of conversation unwound
as we slowly rolled the floss
of autumn pageantry,
then began to weave once more
frail lustrous threads
into the separate tapestry
of our mortality.
Yours is the metaphor, my friend,
and mine a poet's debt;
I had no wish to heed
the waning light,
nor break the sacred
saffron filaments.
"Weaving is an honest task,
fulfilling a human need,
why should I not weave a bright
new design?" I heard you ask,
"Illness and age shall never
quench my thirst for beauty;
watch closely as I now embroider
upon both my tapestries

the tree of life with golden strands."
This afternoon when a truant sun slants
upon your handiwork, laced with gold,
my heart remains impervious
to the touch of winter cold.

RETURNING

"Going home, going home" —
this rhythmic refrain
beats in my blood,
whirs from the throat
of a bobolink,
and sings in the three
repetitive notes
of blackbirds
with badges of flame
on their wings.
There's a total eclipse
of unpleasant things
as the miles unwind,
and I eagerly await
the welcome sound
of mother rejoicing!

A MOTHER AMIDST DESTRUCTION

I wait in wonder —
breathless,
expectant,
trembling
like a nestling
afraid to fly.

Come to me before
the last star
has flickered out.
Come to me before
the dawn has brushed
the face of day
with blood-stained
brush. Come to me
while the missles
still are sheathed
in the scabbard.
Come and enfold me
in the shadow of Your
Formless Form.
Loosen the shroud
of my fear,
Take me and my unborn
child into Your orbit,
where galaxies spin
a silver disc
of lullabies,
and drums beat
in starstruck tympany.

Let no mushroom cloud
enshroud the birth
of my little one,
when he slips uninvited
from the warmth
of my womb
onto earth
that once flowered
with love, and now
deflowered,
lies consumed.

Will my cindered tomb
be the cradle
where he shall lie?
Or will You spread
Invisible wings,
Shaddai, and enfold
mother and son
from the terror
of thunder guns?

I wait in wonder,
homeless,
timeless,
trusting,
and no longer
am I afraid
to fly.

THE POET'S ASCENT

He descended into Dante's inferno
And kissed God's calloused toe;
Then swung the tiger by his thousand tails
Until they both were spun in tawny seas.
Struggling with the bone white shark
His knife flashed seven times. . .
As the open belly rubied foam,
Hunter and hunted were one.
Tasting the salt of blood-stained spume
He crawled from sea to land.
The hearse crept along the shore road,
And copious roses could not sweeten
The scent of decaying flesh.
The mourners keened for heretic saints,
Martyred by the silent meek.
Enraged, he flung the icons down,
The sound of splintering stone rang clean.
Out of echoing air the white elk leaps!
Running, stumbling, he strains to seize
The mammoth horns beyond the reach of hands;
Then the elk turns in hushed encounter,
Poet eyes gaze into prophet eyes
As antlered glances lock.
A moment slips into the clock stream —
Both poet and prophet
Move onward and up!

ANNIVERSARY NIGHT

Once more we cross the trestle of time,
and hear again the echo
of wedding chimes and train bells
mingling in the November air.
Our passing years like freight cars
are laden with cargo,
and all the records of our days,
packed in orange crates,
destined for another planet.
This moving night of nights,
we laugh like truant children
riding on top of boxcars
to an unknown station.
Holding hands and searching
for the Great Dipper's North Star,
we forget our transient fears,
that galaxy — ours for the reaching!